SHAH HUSSAIN

(Madhu Lal)

A *Malamati* Sufi of the Punjab

SELECTED POEMS

To the side of riverbank always
galloping...
Shah Hussain, God's fakir, is
calling...
'For sight of You, I am always
longing...
for a brief moment me You're
seeing!'

SHAH HUSSAIN

(Madhu Lal)

A *Malamati* Sufi of the Punjab

SELECTED POEMS

Translation & Introduction

Paul Smith

NEW HUMANITY BOOKS

Book Heaven

Booksellers & Publishers

NEW HUMANITY BOOKS
BOOK HEAVEN
(Booksellers & Publishers for over 50 years)
47 Main Road Campbells Creek
Victoria Australia

ISBN: 9798353119029

Punjabi Poetry/Indian Poetry/Sufism/Sufi Poetry/IslamicMysticism

For a complete list and information on our over
1300 publications go to amazon.com/author/smithpa

CONTENTS

Hey, you recognise you...

if you get to know your Self, the Divine you'll know.

Palaces and premises you

will reside there, so high O you who so lovely grow!

Death is everywhere, you

are wise to remain here, so under shelter and roof go.

Fakir Hussain says to you:

This whole world, it is nothing, but a passing show!

Shah Hussain (1538–1599), was a Punjabi Sufi poet who is regarded as a pioneer of the *kafi* form of Punjabi poetry. He lived during the ruling periods of Mughal emperors Akbar and his son Jahangir. Shah Hussain is also often known as Shah Hussain Fakir - Fakir meaning Dervish (mendicant) and Shah means King. So due to his extremely humble Sufi personality, people called him The Dervish King, a person who was a King and a Dervish at the same time.

He was born in within the Walled City of Lahore in what is now Pakistan. His father was Sheikh Usman, he was a Kulsara (a clan of Rajput) and by occupation he was a weaver (in some of Shah Hussain poetic rhymes he used his pen name as Fakir Hussain Julaha which means 'Saint Hussain the weaver').

His father, in his early age, enrolled him in a local school where he started to memorize the Quran. His teacher was Hafiz Abubakar. While he was studying the Tafsir, he suddenly went out of the mosque and abandoned the path of ascetic and stepped into the path of self-blamers and became a self-blamer Sufi *(malamati)*, he started to dance and drink in public, some slandered him, and some had faith in him.

Sheikh Madho Lal, the love of Shah Hussain was born in 1575, when for the first time looked at his matchless beauty and fell for him, it was the love at first sight. At the time, Sheikh Madho was 16 years of age and Shah Hussain was 54 years old. Sheikh Madho, at the age of 18 embraced Islam and became a Muslim.

Shah Hussain raised him as his vicegerent and became his spiritual master. Shah Hussain died at 63 years of age and before his death, he predicted that his first shrine will be built in Shahdara (located near river Ravi), 'then after 12 years a flood will appear in the river that will reach to my shrine and then my grave will be shifted to Babu Pura (now Baghbanpura in Lahore; the Shalimar gardens) and my beloved Madho Lal will sit on my seat for 48 years after my death' and it happened as the saint predicted.

Sheikh Madho Lal, for the rest of his life, followed the footsteps of Shah Hussain and completely secluded himself from the world and confined himself into the shrine of his master Shah Hussain and at the age of 73 died and was buried next to Shah Hussain.

Because of his love for his devotee Shah Hussain is often called 'Shah Madho Lal Hussain'.

Selected Bibliography

Madho Lal Hussein: Verses of a Lowly Fakir, Translated from the Punjabi by Naveed Alam, Penguin Books, India 2016.

Shah Hussain Aka Madhu Lal Hussain: One Hundred Mystic Poems Rendered into English by Parvez Iqbal Anjum KDP. (Amazon) 2020. (Mostly, terrible... why bother?)

Shah Hussain by Saeed Ahmed, Adnan Books, Lahore(?) 2007.

Shah Husain, Makers of Indian Literature, by Harjinder Singh Dhillon, Sahitya Akademi, New Delhi 2000.

Prominent Mystic Poets of Punjab: Representative Sufi Poetry in Punjabi, with English Rendering by Lochan Singh Buxi, Publications Division, Ministry of Information & Broadcasting. New Delhi 1994 (Pages 68-79).

Panjabi Sufi Poets (A.D. 1460-1900) by L.R. Krishna, Oxford University Press, Bombay. 1938.

Great Sufi Poets of the Punjab & Sindh: An Anthology, Translation & Introduction by Paul Smith, New Humanity Books, Campbells Creek, 2012.

History of Punjabi Literature, 850-1850 by C.L. Narang, National Bookshop, Delhi, 1987.

Wikipedia article.

Sufis & Dervishes: Their Art and Use of Poetry

It has been said that Adam was the first Sufi and Perfect Master *(Qutub)* and that he was also the first poet as he named everything and so through his 'Adamic Alphabet' (see the *Hebraic Tongue Restored*) all languages were born and so… all poetry.

Sufism is said by many Masters and authors to have always existed since Adam as the esoteric side of each faith that has begun by an appearance of that original Perfect Master coming back as the Rasool, Prophet, Messiah, Avatar, Buddha, etc., whatever that Divine One is called.

Many Perfect Masters *(Qutubs)* were poets and many were not. Many came after the appearance of the Prophet Mohammed and many came before him. But, Sufis and Dervishes were called by those names after he passed from this world. The first 'Sufi' is probably Mohammed's son-in-law Hazrat Ali who composed one of the first *ghazals* ever recorded that essentially sums up the meaning of Sufism and Dervishness…

You do not know it, but in you is the remedy;
you cause the sickness, but this you don't see.
You are but a small form… this, you assume:
but you're larger than any universe, in reality.

You are the book that of any fallacies is clear,
in you are all letters spelling out, the mystery.
You are the Being, you're the very Being... It:
you contain That, which contained cannot be!

I have used both the terms 'Sufis' and 'Dervishes' in this book because some of the poets within called themselves not one but the other and criticized the other, for... during the time that they were alive, having become corrupt and following false masters. Hafiz, for instance, always called himself a Dervish and often when mentioning Sufis in his poetry it was usually to criticise them. During his lifetime in Shiraz there was an extremist Sufi Order led by a false master and Shaikh Ali Kolah who sided with various dictators and subjected the people to a very vicious brand of fundamentalism (see my biog. of Hafiz, *Hafiz of Shiraz* 3 vols. for Hafiz's almost lifelong clash with this false Sufi).

By the 13th Century many Sufi Orders had become corrupt and full of various dogmas, useless rituals and power hungry and hypocritical shaikhs and false masters. Those who called themselves 'Dervishes' then really meant 'true Sufis'.

The first Sufi and Dervish poets composed in Arabic even though some of them, including the famous and infamous Sufi martyr Mansur al-Hallaj, were originally from Persia... he was from Shiraz. From the 10th to the 15th century the vast majority of

Sufi and Dervish and other poets in the region composed in Persian, a few in the new languages of Turkish and Urdu and some like Kabir in Hindi; after that... the languages most used by the most conscious and influential poets were Pushtu, Urdu, Punjabi and Sindhi, as the stream of God-consciousness moved originally from Arabia and Egypt to Iraq and Syria then into Iran and Afghanistan and Turkey and the Indian Sub-Continent.

To follow this golden thread of Spiritual Poetry one must follow the true Spiritual Hierarchy of real Saints and God-realized Souls... Perfect Masters, their lives and stories are to be found in the many books listed below and in many others.

What is the essential belief and philosophy of the Sufi and Dervish Masters and Poets? To put it as simply as possibly... The Love of God, the belief in God in human form, the love and respect for all of God's Creation and to try to not hurt anyone or thing. And of course a belief in Truth, Love and Beauty as the greatest of the Divine Attributes. A belief similar, if not the same as the Christian Mystics and Vedantists and believers in the inner way of most religions.

Further Reading...

The Sufi Message of Hazrat Inayat Khan Volume X: Sufi Mysticism; The Path of Initiation and Discipleship; Sufi Poetry, Art: Yesterday, Today and

Tomorrow; The Problem of the Day. Barrie and Jenkins, London, 1964. (Pages 119-154... after the three essays printed above Hazrat Inayat Khan goes on to talk about 'Attar, Rumi, Sadi and Hafiz).
A History of Ottoman Poetry by E.J.W. Gibb. Volume One, Luzac & Co. Ltd. London 1900. (Pages 33-69.)
A Critical Appreciation of Arabic Mystical Poetry by Dr. S.H. Nadeem, Adam Publishers. New Delhi, 2003.
Sufi Poems, A Medieval Anthology by Martin Lings, Islamic Texts Society, Cambridge, 2004.
The Way of the Mystics: The Early Christian Mystics and The Rise of the Sufis by Margaret Smith, Sheldon Press, 1976.
In the Garden of Myrtles: Studies in Early Islamic Mysticism by Tor Andrae, Translated by Birgitta Sharpe. State University of New York Press, Albany. 1987.
Muslim Saints and Mystics... Episodes from the 'Memorial of the Saints' by Farid al-Din Attar, Translated by A.J. Arberry. Routledge and Kegan Paul, London, 1966.
Kashf Al-Mahjub of Al-Hujwiri. Translated by R.A. Nicholson, Luzac, London. 1967.
The Doctrine of the Sufis by Abu Bakr al-Kalabadhi, Translated by A.J. Arberry, Cambridge University Press 1935.
The Mystics of Islam by Reynold A. Nicholson. Routledge and Kegan Paul, London, reprint 1974.
The Idea of Personality in Sufism by Reynold Alleyne Nicholson, First Published 1923.
The Heritage of Sufism Volume One... Edited by Leonard Lewisohn, Oneworld Publications, Oxford, 1999.
Persian Mysticism by R.P. Masani, Award Publishing House, New Delhi, 1981.
Sufi Literature and the Journey to Immortality by A.E.I. Falconar, Motilal Banarsidass Publishers, Delhi, 1991.
An Introduction to Sufi Doctrine by Titus Burkhardt, Trans. by D.M. Matheson. Sh. Muhammad Ashraf, Lahore, 1973.

Persian Sufi Poetry: An Introduction to the Mystical Use of Classical Poems by J.T.P. De Bruijn. Curzon Press, 1997.
The Drunken Universe: An Anthology of Persian Sufi Poetry, Translation and Commentary by Peter Lamborn Wilson and Nasrollah Pourjavady. Phanes Press, Grand Rapids, 1987.
The Persian Sufis by Cyprian Rice, O.P. George Allen and Unwin Ltd, London, 1964.
God Speaks: The Theme of Creation and Its Purpose by Meher Baba. Dodd, Mead & Company, New York, 1955. (Meher Baba in great detail explains the Involution of the Soul and the seven stages of the Spiritual Path, the role of the Perfect Master, the Creation and the different States of God using quotations from Sufi poets and Masters and Sufi terminology and cross-referencing with Christian Mystical and Vedantic terminology.

Sufi Poets of the Punjab

The Sufis of the Punjab, like the Sufis of other parts of India, wrote for centuries together in the Persian language. They copied the phraseology, the similes, and in fact the whole system of Persian prosody and rhetoric in its entirety. Later on, the Sufis began to write in Urdu. But this Urdu looked for guidance to Persia and was so much overlaid by Persian vocabulary, phraseology, and *jeux de mots* that it was really Persian diluted by an Indian language. The national culture was thus paralyzed and national sentiments and thoughts were allotted a secondary place in their compositions.

It was only in the thirteenth century that the initiative to write in the language of the people, i.e. Punjabi, was taken by a saint of the Chishti order of the Sufis. This initiator was Faridu'ddin Ganj-i-Shakar of Pak Patan (Baba Farid). His example was followed by many, of whom Shah Hussain, Sultan Bahu, Bulleh Shah and Ali Haidar are the outstanding and well-known figures.

A considerable amount of fragmentary Punjabi Sufi poetry, of various authorship, has also been found. A few of these poems contain the names of the writers, but not much more.

The ideal of the Punjabi Sufi poet was to find God in all His creation and thus attain union with Him. Thus union or annihilation in God was to be fully achieved after death, but in some cases it was gained while living. The Punjabi Sufi, like any other mystic in the world, calls God his Beloved. But the Beloved, who in Islamic countries was both masculine and feminine, here became masculine.

In Punjabi Sufi poetry, therefore, God is the Beloved and the Sufi or the human soul, the woman separated from her lover by illusion or *maya*. The Sufi soul at times wails, then cries and yearns for union with the Beloved. The Sufi poet in the Punjab generally refers to three stories of perfect love in his poetry. They are the love tales of Heer Ranjha, Sassi Punnu, and Sohni Mahival. These tales of perfect love which end tragically are popular with all Punjabis. In all the three, the heroines, Heer, Sassi and Sohni, who spent their lives in sorrow, always yearning to meet their respective lovers, were united with them in death. For a Sufi these tales have a spiritual significance. The heroines stand for the Sufi (the soul) and the heroes for God (the Beloved sought), After the Sufi has attained union with God he is no more Heer but becomes Ranjha, because for him all differences vanish away and he sees Ranjha (God) as much in his own self as in the external world. The Sufi poetry consequently is full of poems, songs, and hymns praising the Beloved, describing the pain and sorrow inflicted by separation, and ultimately the joy, peace and knowledge attained in the union.

Source: Adapted from: Panjabi Sufi Poets (A.D. 1460-1900) by L.R. Krishna, Oxford University Press, Bombay. 1938.

Other Punjabi Poets of the *Kafi*

The *kafi* contains a *radif* or refrain that begins the poem and ends it and is repeated between the various rhyming verses in-between (usually two to four) and reminds one of the *mukhammas*. Several of Bulleh Shah's 150 songs or *kafis* are regarded as an integral part of the traditional repertoire of *Qawwali*, the musical genre which represents the devotional music of the Sufis. *Kafis* are common in Punjabi Sufi poetry.

SULTAN BAHU

Sultan Bahu (1629-1691) was a Sufi Master who founded the Sarwari Qadiri order, Sultan Bahu belonged to the Awan tribe who are descendants of Hazrat 'Ali, the Prophet's son-in-law.

Like many other Sufis of the Indian sub-continent Sultan Bahu was a prolific writer. However, it is his Punjabi poetry that made him a household name. His poems are sung in many genres of Sufi music, including *qawalis* and *kafis*. His mausoleum is located in Garh Maharaja, Punjab, Pakistan. Sultan Bahu refers to Gilani as his spiritual Master but this relationship must have existed only in the spiritual domain as Gilani passed away in 1166 almost 500 years before the birth of Sultan Bahu.

His spiritual education began at the feet of his mother, Mai Rasti, who was a saintly woman. She told him to seek further spiritual guidance from Sheikh Habibullah Qaderi. After a while Sheikh Habibullah sent him to Delhi for further 'polishing' under the guidance of Sheikh Abdul Rahman al Qaderi. This did not take long, after which he returned to his own, familiar surroundings.

According to tradition, he authored over one hundred works and treatises, mainly on Sufism. *Nurul Huda* (Light of Guidance) and *Risala-e-Roohi* (Book of Soul) are the most popular, along with his poetry collection in Punjabi... *Abyat Bahu.*

Further Reading...

Sultan Bahu: Life & Poems, Translation & Introduction Paul Smith, New Humanity Books, Campbells Creek, 2016.

Death Before Dying: The Sufi Poems of Sultan Bahu, Translated and Introduced by Jamal J. Elias. University of California Press. Berkeley 1998.

Hazrat Sultan Bahu Poetry: Kalam, Abiat. Translated into English... Free on the Internet @... www.haqbahu.com

Sultan Bahu: Sufi Poet of the Punjab by I. R. Krishna & A.R. Luther, Sh. Mubarak Ali, Lahore, 1982.

The 'Abyat' of Sultan Bahoo, Edited & rendered into English by Maqbool Elahi, Sh. Muhammad Ashraf, Lahore, 1967.

Shaikh Sultan Bahu: His Life and Persian Works, Journal of the Pakistan Historical Society 28:2 1980 (pages 133-50).

Divan of Bahu: English Translation with Persian Text, Hadrat Sultan Bahu... Translated by Prof. Syed Ahmad Saeed Hamadami, 1966.

God's Oneness I realized and Love's fire shone inside me:

You!

In heart it burns brightly, showing to me path's mystery...

You!

Love's fire has no smoke, fuelled by intense desire to be...

You!

Royal Vein led me close, then face to face with Divinity:

You!

Jasmine of God's Name, my Master in my heart planted,

You!

Denying creation, embracing God's reality, me, nourished,

You!

Mystery's buds bloomed, revealing God: I was perfumed...

You!

Bahu! Perfect Master who put jasmine in heart be blessed:

You!

When You revealed Yourself, I was lost in what I did see:

You!

Now union, closeness, don't exist; no path, no goal... only

You!

Love, body, soul, time, space have left, my only company...

You!

I'm now in the All, Bahu; in that, is secret of God's Unity:

You!

Only a mind in tune with soul is in tune with my Friend,

You:

only one taming mind, knows Name of God in the end...

"You!"

Mind can make devout and abstinent greedy and tempted:

you!

God's path, Bahu, is no bowl of pudding, on that depend...

you!

You are inside, outside, always in my heart reverberating:

"You!"

Your love's unending agony in my heart's wound is aching,

You!

Darkness of ignorance leaves heart, You it is enlightening:

You!

I sacrifice me, Bahu, to any realizing, or understanding...

You!

Many pray You protect their faith, few for love's gift pray:

You!

What they want is shameful, what they give up, it I'll say:

"You!"

A creed knows not the spiritual height, where we can stay:

You!

"Keep my love fresh! I'll pawn my faith for..." I, Bahu say:

"You!"

If all my body had eyes, tirelessly I'd look at my Master:

You!

If each pore was a million eyes: some close, others open for

You!

Even then my thirst to see might still be: what else to offer

You?

Haj a million times, Bahu, is worth glimpse of the Master:

You!

You're inside and out, all-pervading; where's Bahu finding

You?

You Bahu, wounded heart, your own soul was torturing...

you!

With austerity and worshipping, millions of books reading,

you:

Bahu, were 'wise'; but, the name 'Dervish', is only fitting

You!

False prophets who weren't disciples, connive to get one:

you!

They seem holy but swindle money and things of everyone:

you!

Into gross game of love they fall, not fearing wrath of One:

You!

Bahu says, "On Judgement Day you'll regret such action,

you!"

Jasmine of God's Name, my Master sowed in my heart...

You,

teaching me how to captivate charming Beloved's heart...

You!

He makes me obey, eternally thinks of me, we're not apart.

You,

Bahu, receive wisdom as you are moulded into His Heart:

You!

Bahu's heart's garden blooms so, it shames narcissus too:

You,

in me is holy *Kaaba,* pure love brings joy to heart, through

You!

I circle my inner *Kaaba,* longing for Beloved's presence, to

You!

Veil lifts, *haj* done: way of mercy, through You will ensue:

You!

Learning 'everything', great scholars don't know the One:

You!

Learning Oneness they found essence of everything: One,

You!

God's radiance lights all fourteen realms: blind see none...

you!

If no union with God is, Bahu, learning is smoke over Sun:

You!

BULLAH SHAH

Bulleh Shah (1680-1758) was a Sufi poet who composed in Punjabi, Bulleh Shah settled in Kasur, now in Pakistan. His spiritual master was Shah Inayat Qadiri of Lahore.

The ancestral village of Bulleh Shah was Uch Gilaniyan in Bahawalpur, now a part of Pakistan, though his ancestors had migrated from Bukhara in modern day Uzbekistan. From there his family first shifted to Malakwal (Multan District, Pakistan) and then to Pandoke... that is about 14 miles southeast of Kasur. Bulleh's real name was Abdullah Shah, but Bulleh was his nickname at home, and that is the name he chose to use as a poet. His was a voice against the injustices of the times that were full of hypocrisy and upheavals... criticising the religious hierarchy.

His father being a highly religious person. Bulleh wrote primarily in Punjabi (that is written in the Persian script), but also in the locally spoken language, Siraiki, which is considered a dialect of Punjabi. He was influenced by the poems of Hafiz, Rumi, Jami, Sadi and Kabir and the earlier Sufi poets who wrote in Arabic. His main style of poetry is called *Kafi,* that was already an established form with the Sufis who preceded him. It contains a *radif* or refrain that begins the poem and ends it and is repeated between the various rhyming verses in-between and reminds one of the *mukhammas.*

Several of his 150 songs or *kafis* are regarded as an integral part of the traditional repertoire of *qawwali,* the musical genre which represents the devotional music of the Sufis. *Kafis* are common in Punjabi Sufi poetry… the main exponents of Sufi verse in Punjabi being Baba Farid or Sheikh Farid-ud-din (12th century), Shah Husain (1538-1599), Sultan Bahu (1629-1691), Shah Sharaf (1640-1724). Those following him were Ali Haider (1690-1785), Hashim Shah (1735-1843) and others in the 17th and 18th centuries.

The tomb of Bulleh Shah is in Kasur and he is held in reverence by all Sufis of India and Pakistan.

Further Reading…

Divan of Bulleh Shah: Selected Poems, Translation & Introduction by Paul Smith, New Humanity Books, Campbells Creek, 2016.
Sayin Bulleh Shah, edited by Sodhi Hazara Singh, Pokhar Das, Shikapur.
Sufis, Mystics and Yogis of India by Bankey Behari, Bombay, Bharatiya Vidya Bhavan, 1962. (Pages 121-142).
Sain Bulleh Shah: The Mystic Muse. Abhinav Pub. New Delhi. 2004.
Bulleh Shah: The Love-Intoxicated Iconoclast. J.R. Puri, T.R. Shangari. Radha Soami Satsang Beas, 1986.
Bulleh Shah: Mystic Poet of Punjab. C.F. Osborne, R.K. Lajwanti, A. Rauf Luther. Sh. Mubarak Ali, Lahore, 1892.
Sufi Thought: Its Development in Panjab and its Impact on Panjabi Literature from Baba Farid to 1850 A.D. by S.R. Sharda. Munshiram Manoharlal Publishers, New Delhi 1974.

In a dot, all of the mystery is worked out...
on the dot meditate, forget everything too;
the door on Nothing close, do nothing too:
escape hell's agony, grave's torturing too;
heart's favourite dreams be removing too:
it's the right way problems are tossed out.
In a dot, all of the mystery is worked out...
you rub forehead on the ground uselessly,
long marks can be seen on it for all to see...
you recite prayers and people laugh visibly,
you attend to the outer... not the Reality:
would Truth be covered, not allowed out?
In a dot, all of the mystery is worked out...
From the *hajj* man returns, a pilgrim to see,
their stylish blue robes they wear, you see?
Their *hajj* is used, they sell it... a few see!
Such an act who can appreciate? You see?
Is a truth never allowed to be blurted out?
In a dot, all of the mystery is worked out...
Seek a Master, God's man who stays, be;
in ecstasy, fearless, detached... always be;
no wants, no ambitions, like castaways be:
one with a clean, pure heart, who obeys, be.

Bulleh says, "Truth cannot be locked out!"
In a dot all of the mystery is... worked out!

I... am not knowing, who am I?
Not a believer to mosque going;
nor in the temple... unbelieving.
I'm not pure, I am not sinning;
Pharaoh, Moses, I'm not being.
I... am not knowing, who am I?
Not found if in Vedas sought,
never by any intoxicant bought,
nor by what a drunkard taught,
I... am not knowing, who am I?
Not asleep, or staying awake...
I don't woo joy, the sad forsake:
don't do good, the bad not take,
earth, air, water, me don't make:
I... am not knowing, who am I?
I'm of no country, India or other:
I'm not in village or city dweller,
no Mogul, Indian, Turk neither,
not centre, circumference either,
I... am not knowing, who am I?

Know now secret of spirituality,
that Adam and Eve birthed me:
I've not any name, essentially...
I'm in no house, or wild country:
I... am not knowing, who am I?
I'm in the beginning, I'm at end:
only on me, this One, I depend;
no one is wiser than I, I contend
that I'm Bulleh now, in the end:
I... am not knowing, Who am I?

Your love, has made me dance, madly!
By this... my in love with You falling,
it was like I had poison been sipping.
Healer, I'm sad... me You're forsaking!
Your love, has made me dance, madly!
Sun has gone down, only flush to see:
I'd give up life to see You momentarily.
Mistake was You asked, came not me:
Your love, has made me dance, madly!
From love's path don't me be stopping:
who can hold back a boat now moving?
Hey stupid, see the crew I am joining?

Your love, has made me dance, madly!
A peacock is calling in grove of desire:
love, where is its direction, its *Kaaba?*
After stabbing me, You asked? Never!
Your love, has made me dance, madly!
Bulleh, at the door of Inayat is sitting,
who me in red and in green is dressing:
the moment I left; me, he was catching!
Your love, has made me dance, madly!

One... who the ultimate love is finding,
is singing: out of tune... keeps dancing!
That one who has worn love's garment,
from up above to him blessings are sent.
The moment he, the cup of love's bent,
he doesn't question, no 'no' is receiving.
One... who the ultimate love is finding,
is singing: out of tune... keeps dancing!
That One who keeps the lover in heart,
sets up for that one a life from all apart.
Not caring for music nor for rhyming...
for pleasure with them keeps on playing.
One... who the ultimate love is finding,

is singing: out of tune... keeps dancing!
Bulleh has come to town of his Master,
all the false notes have now gone under.
He talks the truth only to the true lover:
who the bliss of the beautiful is having.
One... who the ultimate love is finding,
is singing: out of tune... keeps dancing!

This love has caused me to be forgetting
prayers and fasts... on pilgrimages going!
The second that One did come... I heard,
it struck an unstruck melody, no word...
and then I gave away my daily spinning!
This love has caused me to be forgetting
prayers and fasts... on pilgrimages going!
That day that One came into my abode,
I ignored all of what the religions forbade
and I was tossing away that heavy load!
This love has caused me to be forgetting
prayers and fasts... on pilgrimages going!
I am seeing that One in every face I see,
I see people do not see Him... obviously:
here and over there all is His... divinely.

This love has caused me to be forgetting
prayers and fasts... on pilgrimages going!

Love is always new... and fresh too.
The day love's lesson I was learning
the mosque and fasts I was fearing...
I saw a temple and it I was entering,
where many drums struck I did view.
Love is always new... and fresh too.
Of reading Vedas and Koran I tired,
head bald from all kneeling required,
to Mecca or Mathura He's not fled;
only he who found Him can tell you:
Love is always new... and fresh too.
Prayer-mat burn and water pot break,
give up the rosary, the staff forsake.
Lover, shout as loud as ears can take:
"Leave prescribed... eat what is true;
Love is always new... and fresh too."
Heer and Ranjha* have met already;
she looks in orchard, unsuccessfully!
Ranjha's now lying in her arms, see?

Now she has him, he's full too... true

Love is always new... and, fresh too!

**Note: The Punjabi Sufi poets use the lovers Heer and Ranjha and Sohni and Mahiwal like the Persian poets use Layla and Majnun and Farhad and Shirin as symbols of human love sublimated into spiritual love.*

O my Beloved, come, of me take care, I am in much agony!
Always apart, boring dreams, seeking You, eyes tired be:
in desert alone I'm robbed, wayward gang waylaying me!
Clergy and judge show the way, a maze that amazes all:
the age's real thieves, with a net of holy crime to enthral!
With old-fashioned unreal ways, they tie my feet tightly!
Caste, creed my love rejects; from rituals, dogmas, I flee!
Master lives on far off bank, as wind of greed catches me.
Boat anchored, He waits; if I'm not late, I'll have to hurry!
Bulleh has to find Beloved and should never frightened be:
Beloved's so near yet in bright daylight seeking Him is he.
O my Beloved, come, of me take care, I am in much agony!

Our own creation, is all of this confusion.
Why, frightened of the truth must you be?
Only truth can get you through, smoothly!
Truth helps one to fight... grow naturally.
It is often strange, but it is always spot on!
Our own creation, is all of this confusion.
He, is closer to us than the jugular vein...
this confusion comes from people, so vain.
Who could end the old way they complain?
To find a solution is time spent all in vain!
Our own creation, is all of this confusion.
Bulleh takes love's path, road without end.
Blind meets the blind... who to away send?

Forget everything else, and understand One!
Ways of separate thinking throw off you one
who is being led into hell, torture of any one,
flush out your mind of being, a helpless one!
This argument, goes one and on and on and
yet, it is still all inside that One, contained!
Some kind of use bowing one's head... has?
All this prostrating, somewhere led... has?
Repeating "There is no god, but God" has?

Reading *Koran,* but not the one Word, has?
Truth has to be now and forever sustained...
yet, it is still all inside that One, contained!
Ascetics, they go into the forest... so what?
Others only one grain they digest, so what?
On the wrong path they're a pest, so what?
They return, alive or dead at best, so what?
They are so thin and in a yogic position led:
yet it is still all inside that One, contained!
Look for Master, pray and to God surrender:
that, will be leading you, to real surrender...
and with the Lord you will really surrender...
this is the truth, Bulleh now does surrender:
yet, it is still all inside that One, contained!

KHWAJA FARID

Khwaja Ghulam Farid (1845-1901) was the son of Khwaja Khuda Bakhsh. His mother died when he was five years old and he was orphaned at age twelve when his father died. He was educated by his elder brother, Fakhr Jahan Uhdi.

He was a scholar and wrote several books. He knew Arabic, Persian, Urdu, Sindhi, Punjabi, Braj Bhasha, and Seraiki. It is said that when Farid was a child Maulana Muhammad gave him the first lesson of the alphabet and asked him to say... "Alif". He repeated it until everyone present went into a trance. Some *qawali* singers were invited and they recited the same word on their musical instruments. The trance remained for a considerable time.

At eight he had memorised the *Koran.* At thirteen he became the disciple of his elder brother. When he was 28 his brother died. Farid left for Ruhi where he remained for about eighteen years. It was a wilderness, but suitable for a recluse. This wilderness is often mentioned in his poems.

The poems of Farid speak of the sadness of his separation from God and Prophet Muhammad. At times he felt great separation and sang in his ecstasy of love which united him to his creator but with a veil in between them. The shortest way to the creator is Love, and he used this method of attaining sublimation. Khwaja

Ghulam Farid was the last great Sufi poet of the Punjabi language. He composed over 270 *kafis* that are full of the love of God. Some say that Punjabi Sufi poetry reaches its ultimate climax in his *kafis*.

Further Reading...

Prominent Mystic Poets of Punjab: Representative Sufi Poetry in Punjabi, with English Rendering by Lochan Singh Buxi, Publications Division, Ministry of Information & Broadcasting. New Delhi 1994 (Pages 122-143).
Fifty Poems of Khwaja Ghulam Farid, Translated by Christopher Shackle. Basm-e-Saqafat, Multan 1983.
Teachings of Khwaja Farid by Christopher Shackle. Bazm-e-Saqafat, Multan 1978.
Message of Diwan-i-Farid, Shahzad Qaiser, Suhail Academy, Lahore, 2009.
The Metaphysics of Khawaja Gulam Farid by Shahzad Qaiser, Bookhome, 2020.

With the *musag*-root my teeth I kept shining,
I wasted all day;
with some makeup myself I kept beautifying,
I wasted all day.
I lined eyes with eyeliner, lipstick reddened lips... straight away;
ready for love, I scared off crows, Beloved never came to stay!
In jungle, desert, Ruhi's wilderness for my love I went, far away:
I never slept well for a moment, such a fate never came my way!
In God's Name I unveiled and Love's burden then held sway...
Ranjha* is mine, I'm His: it's in fate's book from the First Day!
O Farid, separation is too long, I am almost ashes, blown away!

**Note: Ranjha... The Beloved, God.*

We have to leave this world some evening or morning:
the house will stay empty... birds are soon migrating.
House a delusion, country foreign, land an alien thing.
There is no comrade or companion, grief to be sharing.
If it had not been pre-ordained, who would be coming?
From that Place of Spiritual Beauty, I was ascending!
O Lord, a glimpse of that separated lover I'm seeking.
Farid, the pangs of separation can be most annoying...
all of my life, much misfortune has me, been following!

My friend, faith, religion and longing
You are:
my body, spirit and soul, heart loving,
You are!
The direction to which I am praying...
You are:
Mecca, mosque, pulpit for preaching
You are.
My *Koran*, my holy books for reading,
You are.
The religious obligations I am doing...
You are.

Haj, charity, call to prayer, fasting...

You are!

My asceticism and my worshipping...

You are;

my obedience and all this pious living,

You are.

My knowledge and my understanding,

You are:

my contemplation, my remembering...

You are.

All of my ecstasy and all my tasting...

You are.

My love, sweetheart, honey, darling...

You are!

My soul-mate... favourite; my blessing

You are!

My spiritual teacher who is guiding...

You are:

my Master, enlightened one, inspiring

You are.

My hope, my wish, loss and gaining...

You are!

My pride, deliverance, all I am seeing,

You are!

My faith, honour, modesty, glorifying,

You are!

My pain, sorrow, playing, my crying…

You are.

My illness, remedy that me is curing…

You are.

What to me to peaceful sleep is lulling,

You are.

My beauty, fate, fortune, fame coming

You are.

My looking, my inquiring, my seeking

You are!

Henna, collyrium for on eyes putting,

You are!

Rouge, tobacco, betel-leaf for chewing

You are!

My terror, passion, madness showing,

You are.

All of my lamentations and my crying,

You are!

My Alpha and my Omega I'm saying:

You are!

My inner, outer, hidden, manifesting...

You are!

Beloved, if You accept Farid... my King

You are!

Kafis of Shah Hussain...

I've found, I've found, my Sweetheart I discovered...
the heavens, throne, air, water that One permeated.
Omnipotent said of Self, hidden treasure Self called!
Hussain says: A cure for us all, Shah Jalal, this said.

Home-girls, Hussain's a poor weaver; greed, lust

has neither...

has been engaged or married or both embracing,

has... neither!

Possessing household or a travelling vagabond...

has neither...

been good Muslim or been an infidel gone astray

has neither!

What has happened too good, for one to say right

has neither!

Leave all lying and cheating and turn to the Divine One...

Many tricks are in act of deceit, you'll weep one day, one!

Difficult ravine, tricky pass, time to realise, stop this one...

stop being arrogant, try to be humble; at dawn sleeps one?

River floods, boat's sail loose, a sailor's taking load of one...

Fakir Hussain says: All doomed, come what may, be One! *

**Note: A fakir is an Islamic term traditionally used for Sufi Muslim ascetics who renounce their worldly possessions and dedicate their lives to worship God. They do not necessarily renounce all relationships and take a vow of poverty, some may be poor and some may even be wealthy, but the adornments of the temporal worldly life are kept in perspective and do not detract from their constant neediness of God.*

Body and soul torn to pieces, you're not attracted Friend?

We've no excuse or apology whatever is offered at end!

Hussain, God's fakir, says: But for You I have no friend...

You're wise with foresight, pride of helpless in the end!

Befitting Friend's hospitality we heart's blood
filtering are...
liver removing, tearing it to bits, even if it doesn't suit
You!
Nothing else to offer, but, we a cup of water
offering are...
I lay in bed to sleep, but... I fell, dead into separation
anew!
A letter to You: know how heart's words a
scribbling are...
hard nights, despairing days, Your ruthless looks kill
too!
If You turn back to look see hopeless those
despairing are!
Beloved, whatever's the way wanted, desire's old not
new!
Night and day You are in focus, we drifting,
floating are...
thanks to You I roam free, on foot seeking the woods
anew!
I never stop crying as eyes implore... us You
faulting are?

Pains and thorns are an evil; no in-laws, father being
untrue!
There is no hope of You alone to us to shore,
pulling are?
Hussain, fakir of God, says: Those pains are odd to
you?
For us it's a burden; beyond this, we truth
knowing are!

This living world implores Ram and is asking:

'Give mortar, pestle, hemp, space for mashing.

Give a duster, chilies, colour... without asking!

Give a poppy, box, clay jug, sugar containing.

Give intuition, insight... hermit to be knowing!

Hussain, God's fakir, it's a dervish imploring!

For a while you think of heart, a means of
getting one!
Man was made to say God's name but rotten are
you!
Heart, face, different; world's a dying, now
living one!
Shah Hussain, sees world as moving caravan, for
you.

Hey, you recognise you...

if you get to know your Self, the Divine you'll know.

Palaces and premises you

will reside there, so high O you who so lovely grow!

Death is everywhere, you

are wise to remain here, so under shelter and roof go.

Fakir Hussain says to you:

This whole world, it is nothing, but a passing show!

Hey, lady, of small worth your grace, O beautiful thing:

I find in flowerbeds jasmine, roses bloom, a dusty sapling!

All the world is a lie, pride is false, the world isn't knowing...

Hussain's wise words: Less arrogance, humility be having!

Do not sleep at all, now keeping on
weeping be...
as flesh, bones, sigh from pain, body
wailing be!
Upon a bed of thorns, no comfort in
sleeping be...
clothes got all muddy, when will any
washing be?
With You lies cure for pain, doctor be
letting be...
Hussain, fakir of God says: Let fate
coming be!

No one will ever be returning to the earth again;
never forever blooms rose, nor the months of rain.
Years of youth are only a few days, never to gain;
so what's it that makes these acts of deceit plain?
One is with father for days, then in-laws in pain.
Hussain says: In woods be buried to settle again!

One is talking of moving, departing, not to live here...

hey, all you own is six feet of earth, your grave's all!

Golden shades on high temples, a way out... to fall...

any wealth you're proud of is source for foes to recall!

You came here with soul, now go as destiny did call...

after destiny calls for actions you have to do it... all!

Hussain, God's fakir, says: Leave world, do not stall...

hey, hear this... die before your death, this... now hear!

Awhile light is seen of those living, dead are not noticed...

all four carried the lounge chair, to in-laws they proceeded.

Mother and sister-in-law, me bride of no dowry mocked!

Some went to graves quickly, God's retribution faced...

there was prevailing the news of being afraid... disgraced!

Hussain, fakir, says: To leave the world one is forced!

One day, alleys of fathers by like dreams would be flashing...

wasps fly off the flowers and fruit, leaves they are leaving!

I searched the woods, the riverside every plant and sapling...

women worked on spinning wheels, after married... going!

At night women gave over to love, husbands were moving...

fire of love bodies experienced, sweet was all that whispering!

Hussain, God's fakir, says: Sweet separation, I'm burning!

Now, giving advice to all those crazy acting

we are...

drugs bought don't work, wise doctor asking

we are.

Dark went, light here, for time gone, crying

we are!

Five rivers before us, fallen sailor blaming

we are?

Hussain, fakir, says: God's will, failing...

we are!

O my dear soul, time to spin reels is going
quickly...
wind spins at night, in corner weft, warp...
lonely!
If a warp isn't right, boss is not pleased or
happy!
For a few days, living like cuckoo, wake up
heavenly...
death is soon, don't relax; rich, poor do not
see!
To those new and old and to those not but
free
Hussain, fakir, says: Without excuse pass,
openly!

Arm around neck of loved one, why be releasing

me?

Like poppy for addicted, it in bones was moving

me!

Without repeating Ram's name, tasting living...

me?

Hussain: Get to the Divine Being, I'm saying...

me!

I grieve so... my love make me come across, I'm delirious...

I ask for no dowry from father, from mother no compassion.

Ranjhan's the one I call, so Herr has no more confusion...*

weeping in bridal bath, forced into a wedding occasion.

Married to angry Khaida, weeping, wailing, forgotten!

All night hanging around, sides on thorns... wriggling;

patiently serve, lure, Ranjhan, Heer dreams conceiving!

As night darkens, buffaloes blacken, to river moving.

Fakir Hussain says: May God, separated be joining.

**Note: In Punjabi folk and Sufi poetry Herr and Ranjhan are two unlucky lovers like Layla and Majnun in Arabic and Persian poetry whose love rises from human to divine love. Shah Hussain has many poems about them.*

You women make no mistake, what if mistaken

I am?

Drinking love of the Avatar, having mind taken

I am!*

Leaving world's honour, departing side of One,

I am!

Fakir Hussain says: By Your Name, drunken...

I am!

**Note: 'Avatar' or God in human form as with Adam, Zoroaster Rama (Ram), Krishna, Buddha, Jesus. Hussain usually means Ram or Rama (about 3500 B.C.)*

O woman, finally you'll be sad; darling, to lure be rising...

that red and green dress, you cater for dreams or wishes!

Just be a spouse, not loving, liking, let work those colours...

all of those girls of your age in dust and earth are walking!

Where have those youthful years gone, all beauty vanishes...

where are pomp, pride and spouse; all myth, story telling?

Where's all your gold, silver... all in the dust that washes?

Where bridal jewels, pearls, looks, folks that are coming?

Poor fakir Hussain says: The path be taking of spouses!

Spouse, it is the time to please you, wake up if asleep...

on your shoulders two angels good and bad are writing.

Hey girl, if you don't make the time there'll be suffering!

Hussain says: Spouse is asking, how are you responding?

Sun sets as daytime falls, no turns of water-well's

pulley...

girls, be home in the light, fake work doing do not

be!

Some buckets filled, some to fill, late it's getting...

quickly;

hey girls, you'd regret it if taken by whirlpool you

be!

Hussain, God's fakir, says: You'd never return...

obviously!

Ah my dear friend, you may to the One know
closeness....
those close are proud, us naked are proud of
nakedness!
Us naked in the world people laugh at such
openness...
Hussain, fakir, says: Providence knows all
truthfulness.

Crying and wailing loudly, I am sweetheart of

Ranjhan...

listen folks, do not call me Heer, just call me...

Ranjhan!

Spouse I've been seeking, second to none is my

man.

Hussain says: Thanks to Saints, none... doubt

can!

"Fakir! You'd see the One if you were more humble...
dirty cap, no soap, by stream's bank, you're washable?
God's name! To milk dwarf cow under roof: unbelievable!"
"Brook flooded and left me on its bank, is it swimmable?"
Hussain, God's fakir says: Come, what is possible!

In the middle of the courtyard be done with playing...

for any who God's name repeat that One is coming!

Streams flow in courtyard, boats around are countless...

many are seen to drown and many sailors get across!

Courtyard has ten door out, tenth... a lock on it...

Spouse uses opening and you know nothing of it!

In that courtyard is a shelf housing a window, small...

at night with Sweetheart it's a stage, though small.

Wild elephant in courtyard, from heavy away breaking...

Husain asks: Who can monkey with, if awake being?

Dear parents made the ties, we've not many a
day...
To go with no dowry, in-laws came to take me
away!
O my God! O my God! Hey, God!

Your knots are being opened, without telling...
you;
in death's cruel separation, no brother or sister
too!
Come here girls and bride having bridal bath
see...
single day's celebration, no more festival will
be!
Mother bitterly crying, sister weeping near,
constantly...
Azrael, death's angel, hauls to the sky, poor
me!
One small, dark long coffin, no light or lamp
also...
arm to arm death's angel takes me, I have to
go;

twist hands in regret, sighing, it's time you
know.
Hussain says: Friends all feel sad, miss your
glow!

O traveller, don't sleep with your baggage not attended!

You'd be ashamed if one brawled, wisdom be seeking.

Water flows under bamboo roofs any clothing soaking!

Hussain says: Vain, futile, your life... and it's passing!

Heaven is the protector for lovers and fakirs
too...
meld inner with outer as one, all troubles are
through!
Always be drunk, leave guilt, pleasure; both,
too!
Hussain says: Both never die like world will
do.*

**Note: 'Both'... meaning lovers and fakirs!*

My dear girls, by spinning nonstop I was so
weary...
I left with hand of cotton, liking much your
company.
Crows do more, in a long year spun one roll
only.
Spouse not luring, being a bride, what a bad
destiny!
Good spinning wheel broke down; no more
agony!
Hussain, fakir, says: The world pass away,
see!

Sweetheart, my heart it keeps wooing and
courting...
Ranjha to find in woods or by river I keep
searching.
Buffaloes pass, no lover, in Jhang Heer's
wailing!
Day, night, madness, acacia thorns feet
piercing!
Hussain, fakir, says: Friend, one day is
coming!

Master indifferent, my honour depends on
You...
four folks lift my coffin, me to in-laws take
too!
Thread broke, reel gave out, spindle yarn
tangled...
reeling... spinning yarn reel, crow on bowl
landed!
Dark night, muddy streets we went home
through!
Hussain says: Downtrodden, is word for
you!

By being together one recognising, glorifying

is...

my dear Sweetheart at last our home reaching

is!

Darling so sweet I found, no more searching,

is...

courtyard so beautiful on brow light shining

is!

Hussain: Due to Master; me, Friend seeing

is.

Don't believe or trust youth and wealth...

deceitful!

Having swan a mistake, it was a seagull:

unbelievable!

Kith, kin, gem, jewel, in world one is too

trustful!

Maligning, hurting, backbiting, thugs...

incredible!

Hussain: All world truly hails, of God

knowable!

O my mother, to the Chieftain my account be
telling...
strings of desire all knots, body's flesh thorns
sewing!
O mother, so simple... sinned by birth to me
giving.
Doomed fakir Hussain: God alone all life is
owning!

I'm hung up, suspended, as indifferent is Darling
with one who's sultan of words and faith perfecting.
All mullahs and the judges are passing on advice...
the upright and wise point out path, being 'nice'.
Desire, it has nothing to do with the path, really!
Across the small brook is the Sweetheart's hamlet...
I've promised to get there until there I will get!
I'm imploring the boatman to take me over immediately.
Hussain, the unlucky fakir, says: We're all set
to die, leave the world and then God we've met!

To the side of riverbank always
galloping...
Shah Hussain, God's fakir, is
calling...
'For sight of You, I am always
longing...
for a brief moment me You're
seeing!'

O God, my Friend, You my state are knowing too...

You're within and without, and every opening too!

You're my waft, weft and the rest of belonging too...

helpless Hussain says You're all; I'm nothing, too!

Come on girls, come dance the *luddy:* *
just like the string of a kite, tight, free;
with it we have flown along... happily!
Sweetheart of mine hold string closely;
for that One just a kite is this one, me!
When one lies in grave, repents openly;
if You lay in one no repenting would be!
Says Hussain, the fakir of the Divinity:
all the world's being drowned so easily!

**Note: The luddy is a lok dance in the Punjab.*

In life, the pains of the heart supreme are reigning...
and whoever amassed million in cash are worrying!
To hell with white shawl, dervish coat more fitting!
Those staying with friends are wiser for remaining.
Fakir Hussain says: Folk moved out, not finishing!

Soul of my life I didn't find, so I sigh alone nightly;
my breath's unreliable but shelter on way it can be.
Soul and body separated like leaves fallen off a tree:
Hussain, God's fakir, says: Dawn, rose suddenly!

Time for worship; get up, God be attracting:
after a while goes by, you shall be repenting!
On shore many girls stand so duty be doing:
help one, one's off, one's home, one arriving!
God's fakir Hussain says: Girls, consoling!

Folks, to one on God's side grief is promised:
those with God, love old or new is espoused!
On head love's basket's held, love's hawked.
God's fakir, Hussain, says: I've love opened
and give up my life; to grief, I'm contracted!

If you're a lover on the path of love be a treader;
love's path is like a needle's hole, be a threader!
Pious outwardly, sinful inwardly, called... purer?
Hussain says: If a real lover, you'd be it forever!

It is with the last breath you will know,

my friend...

life can be wasted, nothing left to show,

my friend.

You took goods on credit, now you'll go

my friend!

Hussain says: Losing honour is a blow,

my friend!

Day by day life passed, I remembered...

never;

I was so busy weaving, portion I saved?

Never!

I filled pages; worth ink what I noted...

never.

Clear ponds I passed, palms I cupped?

Never!

Hussain says: Beggar 'farewell' said?

Never.

Deceit and deception are here, everywhere...

any droplet of peace isn't here, it's nowhere!

Hussain, in times of lies be alone, you hear?

Heart wants lover but form seeks none near:

Hussain, those two... how to boat row clear?

Hey you who strut, dressed finely, eating richly,
the lamb for death you are fattening, do you see?
All land that you need is a hole to buried, easily!
So, why go on buying, living on land, endlessly?
God's fakir Hussain says: We're in dirt finally!

The gave is calling you to home be coming;

even king, lord, nobility, can't be remaining.

Trick, hope is to let God be in all breathing:

Hussain says: In end in dust we're settling!

Get ready to depart, we can't always here stay;
you build up houses, tall and easily blown away!
Your real home is the wretched grave, you'll lay!
Of form proud? Like a tree's shade it won't stay!
Stop cleverness, be kind, God fear. it's the way!
Hussain, says: To live, die before death, today!

Life's short here, who has time for complications?
Temples, elephants, wealth all are... temptations!
Mullah, judge, armies of the past, now... illusions!
Friend, this world lasts a few days of disillusions,
so be careful of name that matters, no confusions!
Hussain says: It is all lies told to sell us illusions.

The truth is that it's a world of self-helping

motives...

they come and go, the many are possessing

motives!

Folk to holy men are drawn by conflicting

motives.

Good feed poor, naked clothe not knowing

motives.

None offers water without understanding

motives.

Hussain says: Selfless One is not having

motives!

If, I am good or bad... does it really matter?

All that matters is I am yours... O Master!

Fools say I'm mad, dyed in Master's colour.

You in my eyes, I roam alleys drinking more:

Betrothed to beauty I'm Hussain His fakir!

God, between these knees a basket stays,
I go on with my weaving happily, always!
Body a lyre, veins strings, 'God' I praise;
heart, is content and desire never strays!
I tied me to You, always... Hussain says.

My life, the Master may dye into any colour;
rich are all destined to be... a wandering fakir.
Needle of wisdom with thread of love to wear
stiches all destined to be true friends together!
Hussain says: Ask, a throne isn't here, easier.

Arrogant one, count each breath as a blessing:
you brought what and you will what be taking?
World and its contents are never long-lasting...
stay is short, life's unknown, don't be boasting!
Fakir Hussain says: Finally in dust we're lying.

To resent anyone, life is not long for such;
death's everywhere, it's always too much!
We all have to go, even those out of touch:
Hussain says: Death's rope all will clutch!

The whole world knows I want to meet You...
all I desire is to be with You forever, it is true!
Allow me to see You: Your Name's letters too
I feed to my breath, pieces of food that I chew!
Fakir Hussain says: Master, I'm slave to You!

Dear friend, ever thought you'll die one day?

On bed of illusion you sleep, night and day!

The quilt isn't real, the pillow will not stay.

This wandering soul, for a while will stray,

and then in house of bones for a while stay!

Hussain says: Humility is to God, a way!

We're mere travellers, guests for a moment only:
we leave behind all we do possess, permanently!
Lords of castles go, heads on coins stay... lonely!
None belongs here, lose pride and seek humility.
Hussain says: God's rhythm breathe... deeply!

Ahead are deep waters... how can I get over?
Night is dark, journey's long, no other lover!
With boatman I clash; I'm wrong, he's never!
Who to ask to help me, alone I have no other?
My girlfriends play with lovers, all together!
Hussain says: I cry, I'm just a time-waster!

Beloved, sweet friend, let me be sacrificed to You:
visit me soon, my constant helper, sin coverer too!
I ask of You one wish: increase my wish to be true!
Hussain says: I am constantly filled up... by You!

Kind sir, it isn't so easy the truth to be hearing:
why take truth, when lies in bones are settling?
All hearing truth sparked up and were burning!
Lover burnt veils, envious rivals embarrassing!
Cobras in alleys; unharmed, those God loving.
Hussain says: Muddy-footed bride's dancing!

God's watching over dervishes and lovers too
for they hidden and revealed don't see as two;
they easy and hard, sorrow and joy see as new:
in a delirious state they remain and it... renew!
Hussain says: All else passes, but it's so true!

What is a heart? Think on it momentarily!
Source of life is breath, for you and for me!
Humans need to meditate... not playfully:
you're distracted by heart, lips the worldly!
Wanderer Hussain, life as a caravan... see!

We are joyful, playful, from God high-spirited:
some left world crying others laughed, smiled!
Give up pride, be humble, vanity you damned.
God's fakir Hussain says: Change, be moved!

Never trust youth, wealth, both can be deceitful

too...

mistake to see goose as beautiful, it can be a gull

too!

Family, jewels, gems we're alone in world, a fool

too...

fighting, backbiting, like thugs of all we are full

too!

Hussain, all in world hailed knew God, as All...

too!

Those who with them are finding You

and don't worry...

Lucky are all who stay with You too...

and don't worry!

Love's basket's on head each door I do,

and don't worry...

of Your love I've hole to peep through

and don't worry.

Hussain says: Who find You are true

and don't worry!

"To penetrate into the essence of all being and significance
and to release the fragrance of that inner attainment
for the guidance and benefit of others, by expressing
in the world of forms, truth, love, purity and beauty...
this is the only game which has any intrinsic and absolute
worth. All other, happenings, incidents and attainments can,
in themselves, have no lasting importance."

Meher Baba

Printed in Great Britain
by Amazon